AF428710

LONG ROAD TO THE ALTAR 2

BY: R. D. SOLOMON JR.

Long Road to the Altar 2

by R. D. Solomon, Jr.

Dedication

This book is dedicated to the soldiers of God and those who have gone on to rest from their labor.

TABLE OF CONTENTS

Chapter 5:

Chapter 6:

Chapter 1

I never thought it would be this way… my whole world was turned upside down, again. It's funny how in the midst of a storm you can still find peace even though the winds are strong and the rain is leaving marks on your skin. I guess many of you are wondering just what has me using these riddles talking to you. Let me tell you my story….

You see my husband found Christ two years ago and things have never been better between us. For years, he was so fixated on hard work and reaping the benefits of it. It wasn't until God tested him and I with him not only losing his job and going to jail for two years but also with his addictions that he gave his life back to Christ. I am proud to say that he has overcome it all and he is a great father and husband. However, I am not so sure that I can be with him anymore. I'm just not so sure I can trust him. Let me tell you why…

It all started when my mom wanted to spring clean. Shakir thought it would be a great idea to use our Saturday to go over and help her. It always puzzled me how they became on such good terms overnight like that after he got out of jail. It was like night and day. Yet, I was thankful to God for that conflict to be over. The kids were always happy to go to grandma's and play in her backyard.

"Kir," That's what my mom called Shakir. I have no idea how that came about. "Kir, come pick this box up for me and carry it to outside. It ain't

nothin' but trash!" "I'm comin' mom!" he said.
"Let me finish folding these curtains with
Camille!" "She can finish them curtains, this
box is important!" mom replied. "How important
can a box of trash be mom?" Shakir replied.
"Kir just come get the box!" "Baby please go
get the box before mom has a heart attack," I
told him.

I climbed up to the attic where they were after I
was done because Shakir was taking a little
longer than expected to bring that box down so
I figured they needed some help. "Y'all okay up
here?" I asked. Shakir seemed uneasy. "Yea
baby, the box is just a little heavy. I've got it
though" "Well, let me help you." "It's okay baby,
I got it." He implied. "Baby please," I said when

the box tipped over and some pictures fell out. The whole room went silent for about ten seconds then, I decided to pick one of the pictures up. It was my mom in her younger days with a man I had never seen before. Yet, he looked so familiar.

"Mom, who is this?" I asked. "That's... that's your father baby." I paused because she told me my father was dead when I was a kid. However, she also told me what kind of man he was. I couldn't help but look at the pictures and notice how many features I had of him. So I asked her, "Can I keep some of these?" She replied, "No! Throw them all away! I don't want to see them anymore!" I squinted my eyes and let out how I felt, "You never showed me what he looked like and you never told me much about him. So why can't I have a picture?" The room went silent again. Shakir was standing behind me with his head down whispering my name begging me to stop. "Baby, please, let it go okay?" I took a breath and decided I didn't even want a picture of him anymore. Yet, Shakir's body language and the faces he was making didn't sit well with me. It was almost as if he had seen a ghost. "What's wrong with you?" I asked him. He zoned out for a second and said, "No…nothing baby, I'm okay. Let me get this box out of here." Little did they know, I had already snuck a picture of my dad in my pocket in the middle of me talking. I wanted to know more about him, and I was not about to let my mom stop me. I deserved to know.

That night when we got home after everyone showered, we prayed in our room as we normally do as a family before the kids went to bed. Yet, some words struck me that Shakir said in the prayer... "All-wise and everlasting God our Father in Heaven, we thank you for another day. We thank you for keeping us all day long. We thank you for the blessings we have received today. Father, I pray you meet us in our dreams tonight. Guide us in the ways you would have us to go. Protect us from hurt, harm, and dangers tonight, seen and unseen. Do not allow our past to affect our future Father. Do not allow past events to affect us now Lord. Allow us to continue to move forward as a family. We thank you for who you are and all that you have done. In Jesus' name, amen."

"Daddy, can I pray tomorrow night?" Tristen asked. Shakir paused and tears began to form in his eyes. "Of course son, just say whatever is on your heart, okay?" "Okay, dad. Goodnight!" "Night daddy! Night mommy!" Shakira said. We gave them kisses on the forehead and they went to bed. That is when I decided to ask the question.

"Baby, what's bothering you?" Shakir looked away as we climbed into bed. "What are you talking about baby?" "I noticed ever since we were in the attic at mom's, you have been acting a little strange. Are you leaving me for my mom?" I laughed to try to open him up a little. He laughed and said, "Never baby. I'm just a little tired, that's all." " Are you sure you're okay?" I asked once more. He kissed me and said, "Yes baby, now get some sleep. We both have to work in the morning." When he rolled over, I pulled out the picture of my father just to look one more time before I went to bed. That is when my journey began for the better and the worst.

Chapter 2

The next morning, the kids and I were awakened by the smell of Shakir cooking breakfast, a rare but enjoyable and tasty thing he does. However, he usually cooks when he is worried. So after breakfast, I had already set in my mind to talk to him to see what was going on before I left for work. I was also going to talk to him about what I was trying to do in regards to my dad. He's my husband of course, so I didn't want to hide anything from him.

"Tristen! Kira! C'mon! Y'all are going to be late for school!" he said. I can still hear the feet of the kids running down the stairs and Shakira screaming, "Daddy cooked breakfast! Daddy cooked breakfast!" I got up slowly as usual and looked myself in the mirror, "God, please let it be a good day," I said to myself. Then I showered and went downstairs to join the family. "Mommy, daddy cooked chocolate chip pancakes! Isn't that your favorite?" Shakira said excitedly. "Yes, those are my favorite. Baby, what has you cooking this morning?" I said. Shakir smiled and said, "I just felt like cooking for my family this morning, no particular reason." I smiled and hugged him and said, "Well thank you, baby, I needed it." The kids ran to the bus stop, which was conveniently right outside of our house. Before they left, we prayed as usual and we got our hugs, kisses and I love you's in. That's when I told Shakir to sit and talk with me for a second. "Baby, what's going on?" I asked him. He looked at the table and said, "Nothing baby, I'm okay?" That's when I told him," Well, I wanted to talk to you about something." "What is it baby?" he said as he looked at me in anticipation. "Well, you know what I went through as a kid with my mom. We were all one another had. Yet, I have always wondered what my father's family was like. I want to at least try to find them. I know he is dead, but I think it would be beneficial to find the other side of who I am. What do you think baby?" Shakir paused and took a deep breath. He grabbed my hands, took another deep breath and said, "I support whatever you want to do in regards to that baby. I think it would be very beneficial for you to find your father's family and learn more about him from them."

I could see in his eyes that it was something he was holding back from me. It made me very uneasy, but I could not put my finger on what was going on. It almost looked like he was going to cry. I pulled out the picture and told him, "I took one of those pictures from the ones that mom had before y'all threw them away. Shakir looked at the picture as if my father was so familiar to him, like a long lost cousin or someone he had seen before. The only thing he said after his brief pause was, "You look just like him." Then he got up and walked away. "I'm headed to work baby. I have some pork chops marinating for dinner so don't worry about dinner either, okay?" I replied, Okay, now I know something is wrong. The only time you cook like this is our anniversary week and that is nowhere near now, what's going on baby?

Talk to me. "Nothing baby, I just want to cook that's all. I love you," he said as he kissed me on the cheek. I was left wondering what was really on my husband's mind. Was he cheating? Did he have a surprise? Had he relapsed again? All I could do was hope the home that we had built once more would not come crumbling down…again.

Chapter 3

I tried not to let my concern show when I walked through the door at work, but apparently, it was to no avail to Valerie. We had been best friends for a little over three years now. We ran into each other in a clothing store while Shakir was in jail. She is the one who helped me get the job I have now. When I sat down at my desk, it wasn't even a full two minutes until she came up to me and asked, "What happened girl?" I laughed instantly and said, "Girl, what are you talking about?" "Girl c' mon now; anybody can tell something is wrong with you at any given time when you don't come in with that coffee cup in your hand. Now, what's going on?"

I laughed again and tried not to answer her question by responding with, "Girl you crazy." She just would not give up however and responded with, "Crazy enough to know when something is wrong with you so spill it." "It's nothing big Val. Shakir has just been acting a little out of his norm lately ever since I told him

I was trying to find my dad's family." Valerie sat for a second and said, "Maybe he's just being distant because he doesn't know how to react to something like that, or do you think he's cheating? Do you think he may be gay?" "I stopped Valerie by saying, "Girl, I have to get to work. I'm already late signing in because of you. Take your crazy thoughts on to your desk now." She replied with, "I'm just saying girl, some men can hide it very well. Check on that."

As the day went on, Shakir texted me around lunchtime and asked me what I was doing and where I was going for lunch. We normally meet somewhere for lunch every day. I told him we should go to Maxine's because I wanted her signature sandwich. He replied with a text saying, "Anything for my loving wife. I love you so much and I am counting the minutes to see you again." Things like that always made me smile. I replied to him with, "Are you sure you are okay? You haven't been acting like yourself. There has been a major shift in your vibe and I don't like it. I want my husband back." He replied with, Baby, I'm okay. I am sorry you feel that way. We will talk about it tonight okay?" I decided not to respond because I was starting to get irritated. I knew something was wrong, I know my husband. The longer he stalled on telling me what was wrong, usually the madder I was going to be when I found out.

I decided to text him back and say, "I have work to catch up on here before I leave baby. Raincheck on lunch until tomorrow." I knew it had to be big when he didn't even question why. He just replied with "Ok." That made me wonder. Valerie could see it all over my face now and so could others as well. I decided to take a walk for lunch and just go get something at the concession stand down the street. I took Valerie with me just to have someone to tag along. A man approached us and tried to talk to me. "Hey sexy, how are you doin'", he said. I replied with, "Thank you for the compliment, but I am married, sir." He replied, "That's cool. What he doesn't know won't hurt him, right?" That's when Valerie chimed in and said, "But I'll hurt you! Gon' somewhere! Valerie was on the husky side a little. She was a former athlete who still lifted. Of course, she was a lady, but she was nothing to play with.

"Why do they always go for the married one?" Valerie said. He was kind of cute. If he wasn't so ratchet, I probably would have taken him home with me tonight." I could only laugh and say, "Girl c' mon before you go to jail."

After getting my burrito from the concession stand, I decided to talk to Valerie on the way back to the office. I probably should not have told her about what was going on but I had to vent to someone. "Girl, I don't know what I need to do. Shakir just all of a sudden started acting funny after we..." I paused after I thought about when he started acting funny.

"What?" Valerie said. "He started acting funny

at my mom's house." Valerie immediately said,

"No, he is not messing with momma Eunice!?" I

stopped Valerie again and said, "Val! Really!?!"

"What? I don't put anything past a man

nowadays girl!" As I got back to my desk, I sat

and thought for a while. What is going on with

him? I hope he isn't cheating. Furthermore, I

hope he isn't cheating with my mom.

Chapter 4

When I got home, I walked into the aroma of a

nice home-cooked dinner. I guess those pork

chops had marinated long enough. Of course,

the kids bombarded me when I walked through

the door. "Mommy!" Shakira screamed as she ran up to me and embedded her head into my stomach. I always had to brace myself coming through the door. Tristen came on behind a few seconds later and hugged me tightly. Of course, the two of them fought for a place to wrap their arms around me. Shakir came out of the kitchen wiping his hands with a dishtowel. He still had his apron on from the cooking he was doing. He didn't say anything. He just smiled and kissed me. Then he turned around and said, "Oh baby, mom wanted to join us for dinner. I hope you don't mind that I said yes." Of course, mom and I had not spoken since the day we helped her get the house together to move. It was almost time for her to move, so

I figured she was coming to apologize and ask us to help. She knew we would help anyway, but it was always good to hear her say she was wrong, something she didn't say often. As I got upstairs and got out of my work clothes, I looked at my dad's picture for a second and wondered should I ask mom to help me with trying to find his family. Maybe she knew his mom. Maybe she has been holding back and waiting for me to ask. I could only try.

While I rested for a second, I could tell my time was up when I heard, "Kir, you shole got it smellin' good in here!" That voice was obviously my mom busting through the door, something she was notorious forever since I was a child busting in on us whenever Shakir came over. However, as I went downstairs, I was surprised by Shakir's response, "How y'all doin? Nice to meet you, sir. And your name?" As I came down from the stairs, this tall man in my living room said, "Roderick. Thank y'all so much for having me. You're going to have to let me pay you for that recipe of yours. It sure smells good." "Shakir responded, "Ma, I like him already." Mom spotted me coming down and said, "Camile this is Roderick. Rod, that's my baby girl." As I walked closer towards the two of them in the living room I felt anger fill my mind and confusion fill my heart. He extended his hand and said, "It's nice to meet you, Camile, your mom has told me so much about you." I paused for a second wondering how my mind and body were going to react. I simply shook his hand looked in my mother's eyes and said, "It's so nice to meet you as well." The kids came out of the kitchen and met him as well. Shakira was always the flamboyant type so she simply asked upon seeing him, "Grandma is that our new granddaddy?" Everyone laughed but me. My mother responded with, "Well we will just have to see won't we?" Shakir came out of the kitchen and said, "Dinner is served, everyone! Get it while it's hot unless you like it cold! It's already dead so the choice is yours!" He always had a way to make me laugh regardless of how I was feeling. Nevertheless, this uneasy feeling I felt would not leave me alone long enough to get through dinner without expressing my feelings. Shakir prayed and we began to eat. It was all silent at first. I noticed Tristen just stared at Roderick for a while. Of course, kids do that upon meeting someone, but Tristen's eyes told me as his mother that he was afraid of Roderick. "Tristen, it's rude to stare," I said. "Oh, it's quite alright Camile. I understand how strange I may look to him. I assure I'm harmless little king," Roderick said. I couldn't hold it anymore, "No, it's not alright, and it's not alright that you're here Roderick. I'm sorry. You seem like a very nice individual but," "Camile calm down. I'm sorry about this Roderick. Can ya give us a second?" Roderick stood up and said,

"I'm sorry if I intruded on a family gathering. Eunice invited me so I figured it was cleared with you all. I'll leave now. The food was delicious. Thank you all so much." "Sit down Roderick," my mother said. "Camile, what's wrong with you? You have a husband. Don't you want to see me happy?" "How are you going to bring another man in my face and you won't even answer any questions about my dad?!?" The room went silent. "Kids, go upstairs," Shakir told them.

My mom sat down at the table and said, "Shakir I thought you would have told her by now." My heart dropped as I turned to him. We had the same looks on our faces…scared…distraught…. Shakir said, "You told me not to tell. I figured you would because you're her mom. I didn't feel like it was my place." "Rod, I'm so sorry about this. We have a family matter to tend to. I'll call you tomorrow?" My mother said. "Y'all have a great evening," Roderick said as he left quietly.

At this point, I'm crying and ready to explode. My husband whom I have stuck by through it all and the woman that raised me have been keeping a secret from me so, I yell, "Somebody had better me something quick! What is going on here!?!"

Chapter 5

In the calmest way I had ever heard my mother speak, she said, "Kir, you've been out of jail for two years now. I thought you would have told Camile by now just from your conscious eating away at you." Shakir responded and said, "One thing I have always been is loyal. You told me not to tell, so I didn't. Again, I figured you would since this was something going on way before I even entered the picture." I chimed in and said, "Look, I need to know what's going on before I explode! Shakir what have you been keeping from me!?! I knew you've been acting funny for some reason!"

"Calm down Camile. I'll tell you." my mother said. She took a deep breath and said, "You know I have done my best to protect you and raise you in the right manner. That's why I kept your dad a secret from you all of this time. Now, your daddy is dead, but he wasn't two years ago." "What the hell are you talking about?" I said in a calm angry tone. "Baby..." Shakir said. "No, I need to hear this." I interrupted. "Are you saying I could have met my father?" "I

met your father," Shakir said. "I spent almost two years of my life with him. Baby, I'm sorry but I did not know until I got out and he was already dead that it was your father. I could not bear the pain that would have been in your heart, much like the pain you may be feeling now mixed with anger. Baby I...," "Stop! Just stop!" I screamed. "Your cellmate was my

father!?!"

Shakir took a deep breath and said, "Yes."

Then he braced himself for my reaction. I had

no words. All I could do was walk away numb.

My heart filled with some of the most

unbearable pain I had ever felt. I walked away

slowly with my arms folded. Shakir tried to grab

me. I snatched away and said, "Don't touch

me!" My mom said, "It wasn't his fault. I should

have told you and, "Look, I just need to go

away for a while okay?" thank y'all so much for

ruining my life. I appreciate it. I went and sat on

the porch for a while. So many things ran

through my head. What did I do to deserve

this? What do I do now? What else could they

be hiding from me? Why did God allow this to happen this way? I didn't know what else to do, so I got in my car and I just sat with no destination in mind. Shakir ran out and asked, "Baby, please don't go. Whatever I have to do to make it right I'll…," "You can't bring my father back!" I screamed uncontrollably. Anger and anguish had taken over me. I was a ticking time bomb for everyone in my path. I didn't want the kids to see me like that, I so I told Shakir, "Take care of the kids until I get back." "Baby please don't go," Shakir said. "You left for two years!" I responded. "I can leave for a little while!" I cranked up the car and sped out of the driveway. Where I was going? I had no idea.

Chapter 6

My nerves were just as on the edge as I was of

getting a ticket. My rage was weighing heavily

on my foot so 80 miles an hour on the freeway

was too slow. Shakir just kept calling me and

calling me. I finally connected it to the

Bluetooth in the car and answered. "Baby?" he

said. "Baby?" I didn't answer because I didn't

know what to say. Anger had my tongue.

"Baby, please come home. The kids are

worried about you. I know you are mad at me

and I am so sorry I didn't tell you. I really did

think I was doing the right thing. I know it may

take you a while to forgive me, but if there is

any way we could work through this together I am willing. I don't want to lose my family again."

I finally said, "Let me talk to the kids."

"Mommy?" Shakira said. "Hey, mommy!" Tristen said. "Hey, babies, I will be back soon. Mommy just has to handle some things and I will be back to get y'all okay?" "Okay!" they both said. "Wait, what do you mean you'll be back to get them? Where are you going?" Shakir said. "Just have the kids ready in about two hours okay?" "So what am I supposed to do? You want me to just let my family go again!?! Camile, I've been doing the right thing. I love you to pieces. Don't let this break us apart again." "Bye Shakir," I responded. I

hung up immediately after.

I called Valerie to see if I could stay with

her. I could not trust Shakir at this point, and

she lived closer to the church than us anyway,

so it would not be an issue to go from there

with the kids until things settled down for us

again. The phone rang three times. I was

about to hang up but then she answered. "Girl,

what's up? I was just about to call you." " I

need a huge favor. Can the kids and I stay

with you for a while?" Valerie immediately

responded, "What happened? He didn't hit you,

did he!?!" "No Val, we just need to be apart for

a little while. We will talk more in detail when

we get there. It'll be about an hour and a half."

"Okay girl. Let me know if y'all need anything else. The kids can sleep on the sofa bed and I have a spare room for you for peace." I shed a couple of tears and said, "Thank you girl, see you soon."

I stopped to get gas on the way back to the house. I saw this couple arguing. The man said, "Why can't we just work this out? We both did wrong! Can't we just start over! It's been three months!" The young lady said, "No, I don't know if I will ever be able to trust you again. You broke my heart." "Well, how do you think I feel!?! You had everyone thinking it was just me until you left your phone open and I exposed you!" The young lady again responded, "See, that's what I'm saying! Yes, I did wrong, but you did wrong first!" "Does it matter!?!" the young man said. "Can we just forget all of this and start over? Please, that's all I'm asking." " I need time." The young woman told him.

I felt compelled to tell the young man what I felt, so I did. I walked up to him and said, "Young man, everything will be okay, give her time. She will come back if that is who God has for you." He instantly cried and said, "Ma'am, I am so sorry for what I did and I have been doing right and doing everything in my power to get her back. I love her so much." I could see nothing but Shakir's face when he spoke. I told him," Be patient. She will come around." Not even a minute later, I closed my gas tank and the young lady was crossing the street. I heard the young man scream saying, "No!" He came running after I heard screeching tires. Needless to say, she did not make it. I don't know what God was trying to tell me through all of this, but of course, I was deeply saddened.

I didn't know what to say to the young man, so I said a silent prayer in my head for him and I drove away in the opposite direction. Of course, it was a scare and an eye-opener, but I had my mission at hand still.

Chapter 7

Psalms 147:3 says, " He healeth the broken in heart, and bindeth up their wounds." As I was going down the freeway, I thought of this verse and realized how hurt I really was. I was numb. It was equivalent to that feeling you get when you lose someone and the realization of them being gone has not set in yet. I still could not wrap my head around why Shakir would keep this from me for over two years. I felt like I had no one. I just kept asking God, "What did I do Jesus? What did I do to deserve this? I'm not perfect, but I do my best to treat everybody right. Why is this happening to me?" I guess finally speaking it did something to me. Tears blinded my vision, so I pulled over to let them all out. I have no idea how long I was there for but it felt like forever. The tears would

not stop flowing. From the pain of being lied to

my whole life to the pain of my husband

keeping yet another secret after I stuck by his

side, the pressure was too great for me to

endure any longer. After wetting up the neck of

my shirt, I wiped my eyes and got back on the

freeway. I knew I was not done crying but at

least I could make it to the house to get the

kids.

When I got to the house, Shakir was

sitting on the porch with his head down. I didn't

know what to expect. There was a mug sitting

next to him. I could only hope he had not been

drinking. I did not immediately get out of the

car with the expectation of him coming up to the car. He didn't move. He just sat there motionless with his head down and his eyes closed. As I got to the steps he opened his eyes. He didn't look at me; he just stared off into space. I didn't know exactly what to say, so I asked, "Are the kids asleep?" He lifted his head, crossed his fingers together and placed his chin on them and continued with his thousand-yard stare.

I didn't know what else to do but to leave him alone. Strangely, he already had the kids' bags packed and they were sitting watching tv obviously waiting for me.

I didn't know how to feel about Shakir's actions. Was he saying he gives up? Was he just trying not to argue? Was he saying we were over? It still bothered me to know what was in that cup also. Tristen was nodding and Shakira was so into the cartoon that neither of them noticed I was in the room. "Hey, babies. Y'all ready to go?" They both looked at me and nodded. So I grabbed their bags and we went to the door. Ironically neither of them asked me any questions.

As we were leaving the kids hugged Shakir and told him, "See you later." He still didn't have words. He simply smiled and kissed them. So, after I got the car loaded, I went back to the porch and asked him, "Have you been drinking?" He took a deep breath and said, "No." So, I asked, "So what's in the cup?" He replied, "Tea." I couldn't take it anymore, so I screamed, "Look, you and my mom are the reason this is happening! Don't try to make it seem like I'm crazy!" He replied softly, "I'm not." His tone and demeanor only made me more enraged, so I told him, "I'll let you know when we get there." "I love you," Is all he said back. He still had not looked at me. Only God knows how long he sat on that porch. He didn't move a muscle as we drove away.

Chapter 8:

Silence filled the car. I wasn't sure what Shakir told them in regards to what was going on, so I left the questioning up to the kids. Of course, if he had not told them there would be no easy way to explain the situation. "Mommy, where are we going?" Shakira asked. I replied, "We are going to auntie Val's to stay for a little while," Tristen had a stank look on his face when I said where we were going. "What's wrong son?" I asked him. He said, "I don't like going over there. She's always loud and she's always talking about people." I had to pause for a moment after Tristen said that. I asked myself, "Is this the best move for us right now?"Then I thought to myself, "I don't have much of a choice. There is nowhere else for us to go.

So I replied, "Tristen, I am sure everything will be fine. We are only staying temporarily anyway." Shakira asked, "Did daddy do something wrong again?" I didn't think she would be so blunt and make me cringe with that type of question. " I replied, "We just have some things we are trying to work out." By this time, my mother called my phone. Of course, I did not answer because I was driving. She called a total of three times.

When we pulled into the driveway of Valerie's house I didn't know how to feel. I told the kids to go knock on the door so she could let them in. My mind was everywhere. I needed a breather after so much happening in such a short time. Tears again uncontrollably fell, but I didn't feel anything. I decided to call mom back to see what she wanted, even though I didn't feel like talking.

When she answered she said, "Camile?" I replied, "What?" Of course, response rubbed her the wrong way and she replied, "Who the hell do you think you're talking to?" I had let out a sigh and told her, "Look what is it, Ida? I'm not trying to argue with you. Y'all were wrong." The conversation was silent for about thirty seconds. Then, she just hung up. So, I dried my face and I went

into the house.

Chapter 9

The kids had already settled in when I

came in. I went to the kitchen where Valerie

was. Valerie said, "Girl I was about to come out

there and make sure I didn't have to," I

stopped her mid-sentence and said, "I just had

to take a minute, that's all. I honestly just want

to go to bed Val. We have work in the morning

and it's been a long day. Can we just take your

car in the morning to drop the kids off and we ride together?" "Yea girl, you know I got you." Valerie said, "Gone and get you some rest. I'm going to have another drink before I go to bed."

When she said drink, I burst into tears. All I could think about was how Shakir put that last bottle away and locked it up and never opened that cabinet again. I guess I was in more pain than I knew. Of course, Valerie was concerned and said, "I'm sorry sweetheart; what's wrong? I won't drink if it makes you that upset." "No, it's okay, have your drink. Enjoy. I'm just going to go pray with the kids and go to bed."

I would have to say that the kids were just as tired as I was. When I went to the sofa, they were already tucked in and Tristen was snoring. I prayed over them as best I could, still trying to be strong for them, "Dear God, I honestly don't know what to say right now. I'm hurting. I'm confused. I don't know what to do right now. Regardless of what happens though, I need you to protect my children. Let me be strong for them. I just want peace God. I wish I could just erase all of these memories and start over. I need you, Lord, help me… help me, please. In Jesus name, Amen."

Valerie overheard me in the kitchen. She had tears in her eyes. Of course, I asked, "What's wrong?" In a monotone voice. She said, "Girl, I haven't heard a prayer in this house in over a year. I stopped praying because I didn't think God could hear me. What would he want with someone like me? I don't see how you're managing girl. Your husband was gone for two years and you stayed faithful." I looked at her and smiled. I laughed and said, "If only you knew why I was here." Of course, she was interested in my business, but I didn't feel that my problems in my relationship were her business. So, when she asked, I simply told her, "We are just disagreeing right now."

Valerie poured out the rest of her drink and said, "Can you pray with me girl?" "Sure girl," I told her, as we kneeled right there in the

kitchen.

Chapter 10

I did not sleep too well. My mind was in

a million places just like my emotions. Every

element of me was restless until I had a certain

dream. I had a dream of my father based on

the picture I had of him. I was a little girl and

he was holding my hand as we were walking.

He just kept saying, "Forgiveness is the key

baby girl. You have to learn to forgive. It'll take

you a long way." Then, the dream switched.

I was hanging over a ledge and I was trying to save Shakir and Valerie. I had one in each hand. I tried to pull them both up but I just did not have the strength to do so. Then my dad's face appeared again as he whispered, "Forgiveness" I woke up in a sweat breathing heavily. I was not sure what the dream meant at the time, so I prayed again and asked God for guidance.

Upon going back to sleep my mom came to me in a dream this time. She was old and feeble in a rocking chair. She was coughing uncontrollably so I went to her and asked was she okay? She pushed me away and said, "Get away from me!" That was typical of her anyway so I turned to walk away. That's when she said, "Camile!" I replied, "What!" She said, "Don't be like me." That's when I woke up again. It was about 5:30 already and I had to be up at 6 for the kids, so I just stayed up.

We got the kids together and dropped them off. As Valerie was driving we had a quick conversation before work. "Thanks for that prayer, last night girl. I feel so refreshed. I have a question for you though." "What's that?" I said. "Who were you singing to last night? It sounded good." I was confused because I did not remember singing even in my dreams. "I guess whoever was listening," I said and laughed it off. "Well, I don't know what it was, but it sounded like an old negro spiritual. You weren't saying words from what I heard. You were just humming."

I didn't know what to say back so I changed the subject, "What's up with breakfast though girl? I need my morning cup of Joe." "She replied, "Girl you're talking about a cup of Joe; shoot I need all of Joe, not a cup of him!" We both laughed as we drove around trying to find a place for breakfast before work.

Chapter 11

Work was not as busy as I thought it would be. I was having a pretty awesome day until I picked up my phone and saw a text message from Shakir. I didn't want to communicate yet, but I knew if I didn't respond he would keep sending text messages and eventually call. The text message read, "Hey, are you okay?" I replied, "Yes." "How are the kids?" he replied. "Fine," I responded. He replied once more, "Ok." I did not send anything back.

Around lunchtime, he sent me another text saying, "Can we meet for lunch?" I replied, "No." He replied, "Ok." I paused for a second before I clocked out to gather myself because I didn't want 1,000 questions from Valerie. We sat down outside at this little pizza place around the corner from the job. I didn't feel like eating, so I just had a coke. "Are you sure you don't want to talk about what's going on girl? It's not like you to not eat." Valerie said. "I'm okay girl," I replied. "I just have to revamp and get myself together, that's all."

"Well, talk to me then. What's going on?" Valerie asked. "I don't want to talk about it, Val," I responded. "Alright, I won't try to pull it out of you. I know you will tell me eventually." We sat silent for a little while she ate and I just tried to relax. Then, all of a sudden, Shakir walks up to me from out of nowhere. So, of course, I asked, "What are you doing here? How did you find me?" He responded, "I wasn't trying to. Just like when we met, it was fate. Can we talk?"

"What's going on Kir? How have you been?" Valerie said. "I'm okay Val," Shakir responded. "Can we have a minute alone?" Valerie looked at both of us for a couple of moments then got up and proceeded to walk back to work. She looked back twice. I am not sure if that was to make sure I was okay or if she was looking at Shakir. "Baby, please come home. I miss my family. I honestly thought I was doing the right thing by not telling you. I did just feel that your mom should have told you about your dad. We have been through too much to just let it all end now." I looked him in his face. All I saw was sincerity and innocence. Yet, my flesh did not allow me to speak forgiveness.

I took a deep breath, looked away and said, "Have a good day Shakir." Then I walked back to work holding back tears in my eyes. I don't know if I was being stubborn if I was just afraid to trust him after all of this. Maybe it was a little of both. I must say he looked really good though. I wanted to kiss him so badly.

Chapter 12

When I got home, I sat in silence for about an hour. I could feel Shakir's name in my pulse. Yet, my flesh was nevertheless winning, so I decided not to call him. However, my mother did call in the midst of my pondering. When I answered, I didn't know what to say, so I remained silent. She said, "Mille, I know you don't want to talk to me, but I just wanted to say I'm sorry. You were the only person I have ever truly loved and I didn't want you to have to look at your daddy behind bars for the rest of your lie. I regret it every single," "Just stop mama." I said. Another moment of silence came over the phone. After about ten seconds, I hung up with a long sigh after.

Val knocked on the door and asked, "Hey girl, you okay? Dinner is almost done." I replied, "Yea, I just need a moment." I could hear the kids playing in the living room. They were the only reason I was trying to stay as positive as possible. I was at wit's end with everything. As we ate, Val asked me, "So girl, was he begging you to come home?" I immediately replied, "Let's not talk about this in front fo the kids Val." "Mommy, you saw daddy today?" Shakira asked. I had to take another sigh before I answered, "Yes, now eat your food so you can get ready for bed."

Tristen was very quiet and had barely touched his plate. Before I could ask, Val asked, "What's wrong boyfriend?" He murmured but we couldn't understand him. I asked him, "What did you say, honey?" He exclaimed, "I miss my daddy," as he stormed away from the table back to the living room. I could physically feel my heart sink as he sat there with his arms folded and tears started to fall. I went to him, wrapped my arms around him and said, "I miss daddy too. Don't you worry. Everything will be okay." The sad part is, I just did now know when and how everything was going to be okay. I really wanted things to go back to the way they were. Yet, I needed to heal from pains far beyond what Shakir had done. My mother had bee lying to me from birth. I was not sure who to trust at this point. It seemed like Val was the only one in my corner.

        "Is everything okay?" Val asked. "Yea, we're okay, he just misses Shakir," I said. Val took the Tristen back to the kitchen and gave both kids some ice cream while I gathered myself. The only thing I could think to myself was, "Ice cream… a woman's best friend during depression." I laughed at myself and showered after I got the kids ready for bed. Val sat in my room briefly and we talked. Her last statement was, "I have something for you tomorrow when we get off." I could only imagine what she meant since tomorrow was Friday.

Chapter 13

Work was seeming to go by very slow as the time was nearing to go home. I could hear the clocks over my coworker's awful choice of music. Val kept eyeballing me and smiling throwing both thumbs up. My stomach became more and more uneasy with each passing minute. Whatever her surprise was, I hope it had nothing to do with Shakir. I couldn't take being near him just yet. When it was time to go, I checked my phone right before I got up to leave. Shakir had called me ten times and sent me seven text messages. I tried to hide the smile from simply knowing he cared. "Are you ready?" Val asked. I replied with, " What are we doing Val? Whare are you getting me into?" She smiled, paused and said, "We're going out tonight!" Of course, my question was, "Okay, so who is going to watch the kids?" Val said, "Shakir has agreed to watch the kids." My heart jumped immediately, " No way! He is not watching my kids!"

Valerie responded, "Girl calm down, it won't be long. I just want to take you out to relieve some of that stress. He's already on the way." At this point, I was sick of sighing so I took a deep breath and said, "Okay, fine."

When he pulled up, strangely he didn't get out of the car. He blew the horn and waited. After all of the calls and texts, I was expecting him to at least get out and try to talk to me. I guess he was being the typical man. Men always do the opposite of what we want them to do when we're mad at them. I had no idea what to wear, what to do or where we were going. Honestly, I wanted to go home but maybe Val was right. I needed this night out to let my hair down, even if I was natural.

Chapter 14

Val took me to a nice bar that was just opening downtown. The vibe was soothing and positive and the lighting was perfect to get my head together and relieve some stress. Val immediately ordered us some drinks. She knew I didn't drink, so I only needed a couple of sips before I got emotional. The tears just started flowing down my blank, numb face. Val asked, "Sweetie what's wrong? You could have cried at home. I didn't bring you down here to feel sorry for yourself. I brought you down here to have fun!" Seconds after she said that, a man approached me and said, "Baby you don't have to cry. I'll wipe every tear and put the greatest smile on your face. Just give me one night."

I got up from my seat, looked him square in his eyes and with all passion and rage, I slapped him. "Let's go," I told Val. "What did you do that for!?!" she replied. "I want to go home! Let's go!" I said. Without hesitation, we left.   When we got back to the house, I sat on the porch and waited or the kids to come. Val came out to sit with me. "I'm sorry I ruined the night," I told her. "Girl what are you talking about? You were the highlight of the night! You slapped him to the floor," She replied. As we laughed off my unexpected encounter with a thirsty man, Shakir pulled up with the kids.

I was expecting him to get out and say something to me. Yet, he stayed in the car. Since he didn't want to get out of the car, I went to the car. He rolled down the window very slow but he kept his eyes forward as if he didn't want to look at me. "How have you been," I asked. He paused and said, "I'm maintaining. How are you?" "I'm good," I told him. Then he rolled the window back up slowly and drove away at cruise speed. I didn't know what to think. Was the man I loved slowly slipping away from me again or was he just numb? I told myself only time will tell.

Chapter 15

The next day I decided I would call my mom and formally forgive her. My heart just would not let me go on not talking to her and holding grudges. When I called, she sounded like she had gotten some bad news. With a deep sigh, she stated," Hey Mille, how are you baby?" "I'm okay; you don't sound too good," I replied. "Oh it's nothing the Lord can't fix," she responded. "I'm gon' be okay. Where are my babies?" "They're playing," I told her. "Mama, I called to tell you I forgive you and I want us to work things out. I'll try to…" Before I could get the rest of my forgiving out, she shouted, "Thank you Jesus! You done answered my prayer, Lord!" Just in time!" "Just in time for

what?" I asked.

  "When you and Kir work things out, I

need to sit down with yall and have a talk. Y'all

need to gone head and get over this now. You

done forgave me. Forgive him, before it's too

late." I could not help but pause again. At the

same time I heard Val at the door. It sounded

like Shakir, but I didn't want to interrupt mama.

"So where is your boyfriend?" I asked her.

"He's gone fishing. Hopefully he'll catch us

something to eat because I don't feel like going

anywhere today," she said. This did not sound

like my mom to me. "Are you sure you're okay

mama?" I asked. "You're always up for going

places. You don't sit still. "Yes, I'm okay baby," she replied. It's just one of those days. I'm not your age anymore. We both laughed and I told her I had to go. I was more inclined on who was at the door.

"Val, who was at the door?" I asked. "Oh, it was Shakir. I told him you weren't here because I figured you didn't want to be bothered after last night." "Why did you do that!?!" I exclaimed. "Dang girl, I'm sorry. I didn't know you wanted to see him. It won't happen again. Do you want me to call him?" she asked. "No, I'll call him," I said. Then it hit me. "Wait, why do you have his number?" I asked. "Girl chill, I got it from him because I wanted to make it seem like you weren't here. I

told him I'd call him when you got back."

Something was not sitting well with me and her

story or the fact that he left his number.

          "Give me that paper." I said. I ripped it

into pieces. "Don't ever do that again, do you

understand me?" She had no words. I went

outside and sat on the porch. Once again, so

many thoughts ran through my head. What

was wrong with mom? Why did Shakir feel

some comfortable leaving his number with

Valerie? Why was she so inclined to get his

number knowing I was home? All I could do

was pray and hope for the best. At least the

kids were having fun playing the yard. They

were the only thing that brought me peace that

day.

Chapter 16

I had some serious trouble sleeping that

night. Even after taking a sleeping pill, I tossed

and turned and ultimately just sat up impaired

but restless. My mind would not stop racing.

My mom was on my mind heavily. Val's actions

had me on edge. The kids were a concern as

well because I am their mother and if I am not

okay they are not okay. Shakira couldn't sleep either and decided to come snuggle under me. "Mom, when are we going to see dad again?" Shakira asked. I tried my best not to show any negativity when I answered her. "Soon, very soon." I told her. She hugged me tight and went back to check on her brother. I guess she fell asleep because she didn't return.

I eventually fell asleep myself. It was a terrible dream. I dreamed of Val and Shakir kissing outside of my job. I went crazy in the dream and shot them both over and over again. I woke up instantly, sweating and breathing as if I had just run a 100 meter dash. I was not sure if Satan was messing with my head, it was subconscious or God was trying to show me something. I was really hoping it was not the latter. I prayed again and just laid there until the sun came up. I knew I would drag at work the next day but I had to work if I wanted us to eventually have our own place again.

Val was acting really peculiar the next day. She was super distant but not in a way that was derogatory. I could just tell something was off with how she was acting. She tried to cover it up by being extra goofy and extra giddy. So, I finally asked her, "What's up with you today?" She looked at me as if I were crazy. "Girl, what are you talking about?" she said. "I'm just trying to be as happy as possible." "Usually when people are overly happy there's something wrong." I said. She laughed. "Girl, chill." she said. "Okay." I said. We continued the work day as usual and she continued to be overly happy, dancing in between cubicles and drawing more than enough attention to herself. I eventually just let her actions go. However, the night before still lingered with me.

Chapter 17

The next day, I decided I had allowed the kids and Shakir to suffer enough. Plus I wanted to know why he was so comfortable with giving his number to Val. I wasn't ready to hear his voice, so I texted him to come over after I got off. His reply made me feel some type of way. He said. Are you sure?" My thoughts were, "Don't push it. I am already being nice." However, my text said, "Yes, I'm sure." He replied with an, "Okay." That is when my heart started racing.

Work had never gone by so slow. I was ready to see him but I wasn't ready to see him.

Yet, I knew the longer I dragged it out the more I would be in suspense and the more stressed I would become. My thoughts were everywhere. I didn;t know if wanting to see him to get an answer was selfish or if I just really wanted to see him to work things out. Not to mention my mom said she needed to talk to us after we worked things out as if she knew we were going to work things out. I couldn't stop watching the clock nor could I focus on my screen. So, I turned my phone face down and did my best to complete the work day without touching it, even though I looked for a text from him every 5 minutes.

What am I going to wear?

Should I cook? Should I use the I don't care

approach or should I be happy to see him?

Should I greet him with a kiss or hey? Should I

be distant or sit next to him? Should I even

invite him in? I know, I sound like I'm 15

meeting a boy for the first time. Give me some

slack. I haven't actually talked with him in a

peaceful state in some time. After I got the kids

we went home and I decided to cook his

favorite meal. Val was very helpful in the

kitchen for some reason. She had never been

into cooking before. As the evening

commenced, he called me. I didn't answer. He

texted like I knew he would and said he was on

the way. When I told the kids, they ran around

in circles in the living room until they got dizzy.

Val said, " He'd better come over! We didn;t

slave over no hot stove for nothin'! That boy

better come eat!" I legitimately laughed at her

statement as my heart started pounding faster

than it did at work. I was so ready to see my

husband but I was afraid of how everything

was going to go.

Chapter 18

When I saw that blue F-150 pull up outside, it felt like I was meeting him for the first time all over again. He stepped out so smooth and silk-like. I had to ask God to forgive me for the thoughts I had as he approached the front porch. I put on my teal silk sundress I know he likes so I can have his undivided attention. I didn't want to seem anxious, so I waited until he rang the doorbell before I came to the door. The kids immediately jumped up when they heard it and ran outside. All you heard was, "Daddy!"

I took a second to look at myself in the mirror and make sure my hair was on point as well as my strapless bra. I knew he liked to see my shape in this particular dress so I decided to make sure he saw it if you know what I mean. As I stepped outside, his eyes lit up and I am sure mine did too. Our connection was rudely interrupted by Val however. "Kir! Hey Kir!" she shouted. "How you doin?" she asked. "I'm okay Val." He replied. "You look as beautiful as ever, baby." He said. "Thank you hun!" Val said. "Um, I was talking to Camille." He replied.

" So you callin' me ugly!?" Val said. "Val stop cuttin up!" I said. "I'm just messin' wit ya.

Y'all gone and talk so we can eat. I'm hungry as hell!" Val said as she went back inside. After the kids played in the front yard with Shakir for a while, I told them to go in and wash up for dinner. "Are you going to stay for dinner?" I asked him. "Only if you promise to keep that dress on." He said. I tried not to blush. Then I remembered why I asked him to come over. So I asked, "Why were you so comfortable giving your number to Val?" He sighed. "Is this why you invented me over?" "Why can't you just answer the question?" I asked. He looked at me as if he was disgusted and replied, "I left my number with her because you weren't answering my calls. She told me she would call me when you got in so I could see you, which never happened."

I didn't know how to feel. It felt like he was telling the truth but my flesh wasn't agreeing with my spirit. " I think you should leave," I told him. He looked at me and laughed painfully. He said nothing else and walked away. Watching him walk away was one of the most painful things I had ever done, especially considering he didn't say a word. At this point, my flesh was sure he was messing around with Val. I just had to prove it.

Chapter 19

We as women can be some of the most patient individuals the world has ever seen, which is how I was able to keep my composure with Val and Shakir. I knew they were messing around. All I needed to do was catch them in the act. Everything resumed as usual the next day. Val and I went to work and I acted as usual. She had her usual conversations about the guys that she didn't want and I acted to care like always. I was waiting for her to slip and say something about Shakir, but she never did. Yet, she did ask why he left before dinner the night before.

I told her, "He had something to do" Her response was, "Or someone to do." This was a clear indication for me that she was seeing him behind my back. It took everything in me not to cuss her out. I just blew it off and said, "Girl, chill." We both laughed and finished the work day. When we got back to Val's, I sat on the porch for a while and contemplated how I was going to catch them. One of them had to make a mistake sooner or later. My question to myself was when and how I was going to catch them red handed. Then, the answer came to me. Just wait.… Just wait.

So, for a week everything went as normal. I had not heard from Shakir and Val kept asking had I heard from him. I finally

asked her, "Why do you keep asking if I had

talked to him?" "Dang girl, I was just asking.

My bad!" She said. I apologized because I felt

bad for the way I asked her. Plus, I needed

things to stay good between us until I caught

them slipping. It was only a matter of time. I

just had to hold out. With me not contacting

Shakir, I knew eventually I would catch them

together.

Chapter 20

Val got up early the next morning and

said she wasn't feeling well. She called out

from work, so it was just me. I asked her if she

needed anything and she told me no. She just

needed to rest. As the normal routine, after I

dropped the kids off I went into work. My

conscience did not allow me to focus though. I

couldn't help but think she was faking it. She

didn't look or sound sick in the least bit. Plus, I

could have sworn she peeked through the

window as I left that morning.

        I knew what time Shakir took his lunch

and I knew he usually went home for lunch.

Val knew the same just from years of me

talking. Never give out your personal

information especially when it comes to your

spouse. So, I left work early to see if he was at

the house. On the way there, I could not help

but prepare for the worst. My heart was about to leap to the dashboard and my blood was boiling. This was all from assumptions that I had already put in my head.

      I prayed as I drew closer to the exit. I didn't know what to ask God for in this situation, so I just prayed to see the truth. I know this may be hypocritical, but after I prayed I reached for my pistol and made sure it was ready. I wasn't going to kill anyone, but I wanted to be heard once I caught them in the act. I was not about to be made a fool of twice. This time around was going to be it. I had enough heartache and pain. As I approached the house, I saw exactly what I thought I would see. Val's car was at the house and he was

welcoming her in. I parked at a neighbor's

house down the street and walked back to the

house. At this point, I didn't want to hear

anything. I just wanted repayment for my

suffering.

Chapter 21

I went around back because that was the best place to catch anything in the house. You could see the living room and the kitchen from there. I saw them come back to the living room from the back, indicating something had happened. I also noticed some of my belongings in Val's hand. She looked at Shakir for a second, dropped my stuff and lunged at him. I was pissed but I had to wait a little while longer to see what his reaction was going to be.

Surprisingly, he pushed her off. I read lips very well. Shakir mouthed, "What are you doing?" She replied with, "Don't you want me?"

I couldn't take it anymore. I used my key and

snuck in the back with my pistol cocked. As

they heard the back sliding door slam, they

both looked like they had seen a ghost. There

were no words for about 20 seconds. I finally

let loose and said, "Somebody say something!"

        "Baby, put the gun down." Shakir said. I

pointed it at him. "What is she doing here!?!" I

asked. "Mille, I" Val said. "Shut up! I asked

him!" I said. "She said she was coming to get

some of your stuff Camille. That's all," Shakir

said. My heart wanted to believe him so bad

but my flesh was winning. I started crying. I just

wanted all of this to be over. I didn't know what

to believe. Shakir slowly walked towards me and said, " Baby why else would she be here? You know I don't want anyone but you. We have worked too hard to get to where we are. You and my kids are all I have. Do you think I would throw it away for somebody like Val"

Val was silent. "Why are you here?" I asked her. "Fine, you want the truth, I'll tell you! Camille, you don't deserve Shakir! Yes, I was trying to break ya'll up so I could have him! Yes, I am sorry, but I am not sorry for the way I feel! Camille, I want you and those bastard children out of my house tonight!" she said. "Don't worry, they will be gone in a couple of hours," Shakir said. "Baby come home."

No, I didn't shoot her. However… I did

get a nice strike to the nose in on her before

shakir grabbed me. As I said in the beginning, I

never thought it would be this way… but I am

glad it is.